Zion
National Park

by Grace Hansen

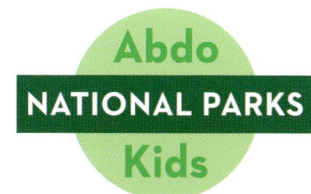

Abdo
NATIONAL PARKS
Kids

Abdo Kids Jumbo is an Imprint of Abdo Kids
abdobooks.com

abdobooks.com

Published by Abdo Kids, a division of ABDO, P.O. Box 398166, Minneapolis, Minnesota 55439.
Copyright © 2019 by Abdo Consulting Group, Inc. International copyrights reserved in all countries.
No part of this book may be reproduced in any form without written permission from the publisher.
Abdo Kids Jumbo™ is a trademark and logo of Abdo Kids.

102018

012019

Photo Credits: Alamy, iStock, Shutterstock

Production Contributors: Teddy Borth, Jennie Forsberg, Grace Hansen

Design Contributors: Dorothy Toth, Laura Mitchell

Library of Congress Control Number: 2018946060

Publisher's Cataloging-in-Publication Data

Names: Hansen, Grace, author.

Title: Zion National Park / by Grace Hansen.

Description: Minneapolis, Minnesota : Abdo Kids, 2019 | Series: National parks
    Includes glossary, index and online resources (page 24).

Identifiers: ISBN 9781532182105 (lib. bdg.) | ISBN 9781532183089 (ebook) |
    ISBN 9781532183577 (Read-to-me ebook)

Subjects: LCSH: Zion National Park (Utah)--Juvenile literature. | National parks
    and reserves--Juvenile literature. | Zion National Park Lodge (Utah)--Juvenile
    literature. | National parks and reserves--Utah--Juvenile literature.

Classification: DDC 979.24--dc23

Table of Contents

Zion National Park

Zion National Park is in southwestern Utah. It was signed into law by President Woodrow Wilson on November 19, 1919.

Nature & Natural Features

Zion is known for its beautiful geological features and valleys. It took millions of years for these formations to take shape.

The Virgin River and its tributaries helped carve some of Zion. The river is also a reason why this area of desert is surprisingly lush.

The Virgin River makes its way through Zion Canyon. The canyon is 15 miles (24 km) long. On either side are red and tan colored **Navajo Sandstone** cliffs.

The canyon is home to many plants and animals. Along the river, Fremont's cottonwoods provide shade. Hidden on the rocks are canyon tree frogs.

Farther from the river, desert grasses and cacti grow. Many types of prickly pear are common. Mule deer and rock squirrels wander the canyon.

Ringtail cats roam Zion's cliffs, but only at night. They often sleep during the hot days.

The Kolob Canyons are in the northwest corner of the park. The area has 2,000-foot (610 m) cliff walls and evergreen woodlands. Here, the bright yellow chest of a Grace's warbler is easy to spot.

One of the rarest sightings in the park is of a desert tortoise. This **reptile** spends 95% of its life underground. It **emerges** in spring and fall for food and water.

Fun Activities

Bike the Pa'rus Trail

Hike The Narrows, a section of Zion Canyon just 20 to 30 feet (6.1 to 9.1 m) wide

Seek out one of Zion's famous hanging gardens

Watch climbers take on the 2,000-foot (610 m) sandstone cliffs

Glossary

emerge – to rise up from.

geological features – the landforms and physical features on the earth's surface.

lush – growing thick and healthy.

Navajo Sandstone – a large formation made up of thick layers of sandstone formed by the sand dunes of a large, ancient desert.

reptile – a cold-blooded animal with a skeleton inside its body and dry scales or hard plates on its skin.

tributary – a river or stream that flows into a larger river or stream.

Index

Abdo Kids ONLINE

FREE! ONLINE MULTIMEDIA RESOURCES

Visit **abdokids.com** and use this code to access crafts, games, videos, and more!

Abdo Kids Code:
NZK2105